W9-AXQ-423

Esquire's

The New Rules
for Men

HEARSTBOOKS

An Imprint of Sterling Publishing
1166 Avenue of the Americas
New York, NY 10036

ESQUIRE is a registered trademark of Hearst Communications, Inc.

© 2016 Hearst Communications, Inc.

All rights reserved. No part of this publication may be reproduced, stored in
a retrieval system, or transmitted in any form or by any means (including
electronic, mechanical, photocopying, recording, or otherwise) without prior
written permission from the publisher.

ISBN 978-1-61837-186-7

Distributed in Canada by Sterling Publishing Co., Inc.
c/o Canadian Manda Group, 664 Annette Street
Toronto, Ontario, Canada M6S 2C8
Distributed in the United Kingdom by GMC Distribution Services
Castle Place, 166 High Street, Lewes, East Sussex, England BN7 1XU
Distributed in Australia by Capricorn Link (Australia) Pty. Ltd.
P.O. Box 704, Windsor, NSW 2756, Australia

For information about custom editions, special sales, and premium and
corporate purchases, please contact Sterling Special Sales at 800-805-5489 or
specialsales@sterlingpublishing.com.

Manufactured in the United States of America

4   6   8   10   9   7   5   3

www.sterlingpublishing.com

Esquire's

The New Rules for Men

Edited by Joe Keohane

HEARST
books

Foreword

There are few things that are as immensely satisfying as a small truth. A short sentence that offers some fundamental insight into our world. You know. Like: Clockwise = closed. Or: Blot, don't rub. Or: No matter how quick or furtive the glance, women always know when you're looking at their breasts. Rules, in other words. We long for clarity. We want simple advice that helps us navigate our world. We want rules. Rules that reflect earned wisdom and experience. Rules that cut to the heart of the human experience and won't be obsolete in 15 minutes. Rules.

That is why we published this book.

Over the last fifteen years or so, we at *Esquire* (*all* of us at *Esquire*) have contributed such Rules to the margins and sidebars of the magazine. Generally, these arise from the lives we lead. Like the time a guy at the movie theater wouldn't shut up ("The dumber the man, the louder he talks") or the morning we saw crowds parting to make way for a man with a hand truck ("Nobody questions a man with a hand truck").

Wherever they come from, however, there's joy and comfort in these little bursts of clarity. We think that joy results from conveying the impression that our crazy world is actually an orderly place, and that comfort comes from noticing something all of us experience but maybe don't ever think to articulate. It could be about work, or women, or food, or travel, or even something as mundane as using the men's room—a lasting preoccupation of the Rules, as you'll notice in the pages to follow.

Of course, some rules don't last forever. Technology, social mores, and world affairs force us to reconsider even the most whimsical codes of conduct, and devise new ones. Which is what makes this entirely new edition of *Esquire's Rules for Men* necessary. We hope you enjoy it.

—The Editors of *Esquire*

CHAPTER 1

THE RULES CONCERNING

THE OPPOSITE SEX

WHAT YOU NEED TO KNOW
WHAT THEY WANT YOU TO KNOW
OCCASIONAL PROBLEM AREAS

Rule No. 1:
When considering uniquely over-the-top ways to propose to your girlfriend, first eliminate all ways that are uniquely over-the-top.

Rule No. 2:
No woman over the age of 17 has ever been thrilled by carnations.

Rule No. 3:

Women with an accented letter in their names are more fun.

Rule No. 4: Wait until after the third date to send her that play you've been working on.

Rule No. 5: Wait until after the fifth date if she's become a character in that play you've been working on.

Rule No. 6: She's going to check your message history.

Rule No. 7:

ALWAYS   SOMETIMES   NEVER

Rule No. 8: Of the various sorts of love triangles, those involving at least one law-enforcement official are the most fraught.

Rule No. 9: Describing yourself as a "hot-tub guy" on the first date will not get you laid. **Rule No. 10:** When in doubt: Gardenias.

Rules No. 11–14:

Signs she might be pregnant

> She wants to know how you feel about the name Olivia and maybe Dakota and Ella.

> She'll no longer ride your favorite roller coaster with you.

> And Jacob.

> Someone named Doula left a message.

Rule No. 15:

The absolute maximum number of times that you can quote Monty Python on a first date and still have a reasonable expectation of getting laid is zero.

Rule No. 16: Of the various types of photographs women insist on sharing, none are more of a consistent letdown than those of her friend's adorable niece.

Rule No. 17: If you're consuming something to flavor your semen, your life has devolved into nothing but a tawdry series of minor amusements.

Rule No. 18:
Swipe right, swipe left:
You're missing out on the magic
and ambiguity of a meaningful
relationship.

Rule No. 19:
But when in doubt:
Swipe right.

Rule No. 20:
No good comes from staying Facebook friends with or following on Instagram someone who broke up with you.

Rule No. 21:
If she dances, you dance.

Rules No. 22–31:
Topics not to be broached during sex

The crack in the ceiling • The thread count of your new sheets • **Possible weight gain (yours and especially hers)** • The funny face she is making • Whether or not the neighbors can hear you • Why the dog won't stop staring • Any current event • How dangerously close that candle is to the curtains • Use of the grotesque in Sherwood Anderson's *Winesburg, Ohio* • **Trial separation**

Rule No. 32:

Any man who pranks his girlfriend for the sake of a YouTube video is not a man.

Rule No. 33: He is an auteur.

Rule No. 34: Of his own shittiness.

Rule No. 35:
A man over the age of 30 should not make innuendoes about things that happen to involve the number 69.

Rule No. 36: Two words behind every successful relationship: *Clear History*.

Rule No. 37: Plans. Then, now, forever. Plans.

Rule No. 38: Nobody makes a sex tape and comes out of it a winner.

Rule No. 39: The only guarantees in life: death, taxes, and the fact that every naked picture ever transmitted via text, e-mail, or app will one day be available for public viewing.

Rule No. 40: That said: How Barack Obama's online, uh, viewing habits have never come to light remains *the* mystery of the digital age.

Rules No. 41–51:
Signs her parents like you

They take down the pictures of her ex-boyfriend. • Her dad starts going straight for the hug. • You are no longer scowled at for poking a little fun at their daughter. • You're invited to birthday dinners for other members of the family. • They stop calling you "this one." • **You get to meet Grandma.** • You're expected to call her Grandma. • When you run into their friends, they already know what you've been up to. • When you ring the doorbell, they no longer turn off the lights and hide. • They let you drive their cars—even while they're in them. • **You get to eat at the table.**

Rule No. 52:

It is impossible to come up with something, anything, that isn't already someone's sexual fetish, shared with others on the Internet.

Rule No. 53: Nipple clamps remain a novelty best left to the pages of *Fifty Shades of Grey*.

Rule No. 54: That said: A little mutually agreed upon experimenting is never a bad thing.

Rule No. 55:
Should your wife or partner
befoul the bathroom: Polite silence,
or possibly an innocent joke.
Note: "Damn, woman, what'd you
eat?" is not an innocent joke.

Rules No. 56–66:

Things you didn't know about women, by women

*TAKEN FROM AN ESQUIRE NATIONWIDE SURVEY

Electronics clipped to your pants are sexy only if you're Batman, Superman, or any other kind of man who needs them to save lives, not send e-mail. • We love the unexpected kiss. Especially the one when you stop us midsentence and make us forget what the hell we were talking about in the first place. • Putting your hand on the small of a woman's back is as potent and powerful as buying her two drinks. Just so long as you know the girl. Otherwise it's just weird. • We like wearing your pants. Not wearing "the pants"— wearing your actual pants. They fit better. • There are pretty much no conditions under which sporting a soul patch is attractive. • We don't want a man more polished than us. Slightly wrinkled and smelling a bit of sweat and a bar of soap? Fantastic. • Despite what we say, you holding a baby with complete confidence is an absolute aphrodisiac. • We are judging your outfit, whether silently or not, from head to toe, right this very moment. • Sometimes we bring you to dinners, parties, and events just to be able to say, "That one is mine." Remember that. • Make your bed every day and change the sheets once a week. That vague goatlike smell guys get will remind us of our brother, and you will be sleeping alone. • You cleaning your apartment is somehow incredibly sexy. Weird but true.

CHAPTER 2

THE RULES OF

DRINKING

IN BARS
AT HOME
ELSEWHERE

Rule No. 67:
Nobody wants to hear about your hangover.

Rule No. 68:
Nobody needs to hear about last night's escapades, either. Drinking is about the present, not the past.

Rule No. 69:
Good bartenders have names like Jack, Tom, or Lou. The best bartenders have names like Jackie, Tommy, or Louie.

Rule No. 70: "Drinking" is everything you do in a bar, including talking, going to the john, and overhearing the conversations of others.

Rule No. 71: Huge difference between $20 whiskey and $40. Not a huge difference between $40 and $300.

Rule No. 72: The heavier the glass, the better the drink tastes.

Rule No. 73: Exception: Drinks taste horrible in mason jars.

Rule No. 74:

If you've been served by one skinny, tattooed, thickly mustachioed bartender, you've been served by them all.

Rule No. 75: Unless that bartender is a woman. In which case, find out her story. **Rule No. 76:** That said, sometimes a bartender's mustache is just a mustache. Usually not, but sometimes. Depends what kind of bar you're in.

Rule No. 77: Premium versions of lower-end whiskey are never as tasty as the baseline versions of premium whiskey.

Rule No. 78:

Nine-percent IPA: Looks like a beer, tastes like a beer. Doesn't act like a beer.

Rule No. 79:
Cold night?
Hot toddy.

Rule No. 80:
Warm night?
Tom Collins.

Rule No. 81:
Pleasant night?
A skosh more viognier, thanks.

Rule No. 82: "Public house"? **Bar.**

Rule No. 83: "Tavern"? **Bar.**

Rule No. 84: "Lounge"? **Bar.**

Rule No. 85: "Speakeasy"? **Anachronism.**

Rule No. 86: "Bar"? **Beautiful.**

Rule No. 87: In a toast situation, drinkers that a man cannot comfortably clink with can go unclinked.

Rule No. 88:

If it's aged long enough, every brown liquor tastes like honey. Tequila, bourbon, Scotch? Honey.

Rule No. 89:
At a place that serves craft cocktails, a drinker may order a second drink before he has finished the first. Logistics.

Rule No. 90:
When in want of a karaoke song, look to 1978.

Rule No. 91:
Talk to the bartender about matters other than drinking.

Rule No. 92:
The drunker you are, the easier it is to pronounce the name of a Scotch.

Rule No. 93: It is not known who supplies the restroom graffiti, but their efforts are worthy of appreciation.

Rule No. 94: When the bartender at the temple of mixology puts half your Manhattan in a separate vessel and nestles that vessel in a bowl of crushed ice and places it next to your glass? That's worthy of praise. Very cold cocktails always are.

Rule No. 95: But then sometimes you don't want a craft cocktail, because sometimes it doesn't taste better. Sometimes it's raining and your flight is delayed and you're 1,000 miles from home, and you just want the lady wearing the maroon vest behind the bar to pour some gin into a glass with some tonic, and you just want to drink it and smile and think of home.

Rule No. 96:
There is no shame in ordering a double
for two dollars more.

Rule No. 97: A drinker should be tended to. If a bartender serving a modest crowd does not ask if you want another drink upon your finishing your drink, then that bartender is a bad bartender.

Rule No. 98:

A drink can improve a mood. Because it is made with alcohol, which is a drug.

Rule No. 99: A bar, however, may not always improve a mood. But it can make it worse.

Rule No. 100:

You can chuckle at the presence of house-made bitters— we all have. But know this: The house-made bitters are terrific. And they improve a drink.

Rule No. 101: And look, they're not going to the trouble of making bitters because they don't care how your drink tastes.

Rule No. 102: With a few exceptions, the best bartender is a smiling bartender.

Rule No. 103: Make your order suit the bar—picky drinkers drink best at home.

Rule No. 104:

If you get even the slightest sense that the bartender feels he is doing you a favor by mixing you a drink, you are in the wrong bar.

Rule No. 105:
How to order a drink

Get as close to the bar as possible in a position where you can make eye contact. Then wait patiently, card or cash in hand. No waving or shouting. And don't cut in front of anyone else.

Rule No. 106:
Water, always.

Rule No. 107: Upon encountering an asshole at the bar, respond calmly. Ask him politely to keep it down. If he persists, not so calmly, but firmly. Never lose your temper. Unless punches fly.

Rule No. 108:
Between now and the next time you're at a Chinese restaurant, you will not drink a Chinese beer.

Rule No. 109:

How to order a drink for a lady you don't know

Discreetly. Ask the bartender to put her next drink on your tab. • When she receives it, politely wave. • **Then wait**—the next move (if there is one) is hers to make.

Rule No. 110:

Leave a little earlier than you want to. Better to be the one who orders the first drink of the evening than the one who orders the last.

Rule No. 111: Before embarking on your Saint Patrick's Day bacchanal, ask yourself, "How old am I?" and whatever your answer is, take off the green derby and go back to bed.

Rule No. 112:

Never pay more than twelve dollars for a cocktail that doesn't specify the spirit brands. Because bar gin is cheap.

Rules No. 113–114: How to get a buyback

Do: Buy a few rounds and tip well.
Don't: Ask for a buyback.

CHAPTER 3

THE RULES OF

FOOD

COOKING IT
EATING IT
ORDERING IT
AVOIDING IT WHEN NECESSARY

THINGS EVERY MAN NEEDS TO KNOW ABOUT COOKING

Rule No. 115:

Give a man carbon steel, cast iron, and kosher salt, and there is nothing he can't cook.

Rule No. 116: Certain things should be slightly heated, if only as a consideration. Maple syrup. Dinner plates.

Rule No. 117: Thighs. Always thighs.

Rule No. 118: Never use the marinade to baste the meat.

Rule No. 119: Because of bacteria.

Rule No. 120: Broiling is generally a great and fast way to cook.

Rule No. 121: It's also generally a great and fast way to fill your house with smoke. Be vigilant.

Rule No. 122:

Sometimes you have to be taught. Ask.

Rule No. 123: A cast-iron pan is not a nonstick pan. A nonstick pan is what you use to cook eggs in— and only eggs.

Rule No. 124:
Toasted nuts taste great, unless you burn them. But you always burn them, unless you're really, really careful.

Rule No. 125:
Not everyone likes tomatoes.

Rule No. 126:
The two "gadgets" you need are a spoon—for everything from tasting to basting—and a cleaver—the sturdiest, most versatile knife on the planet. It works magic, whether you're cutting through a beet or a bone.

Rule No. 127: The best lettuce is Bibb.

Rule No. 128: You have to let things cook. If you're afraid of burning things, you'll be afraid of cooking things. Brown is good.

Rule No. 129: The only way your food (your steak, your skin-on chicken, your Brussels sprouts) is going to get nice and brown is by direct contact with a hot pan. Resist the urge to move it around.

Rule No. 130:

Wine you cook with should be good enough to drink.

Rule No. 131: Because bad wine will make the food taste bad. And because if you're cooking with good wine, you have something to drink while you're cooking.

Rule No. 132:

Always drink while you're cooking.

Rule No. 133:

Relax
when you cook. Don't turn it into a chore.

Rule No. 134:
Tuna casserole is an offense to nature.

Rule No. 135:
Unless you're really good at making it.

Rule No. 136:

Never microwave a tomato.

Rule No. 137: Cheap plastic wrap is never worth the months of frustration it will inevitably cause.

Rule No. 138: Your homemade pickles don't taste better. Your homemade mozzarella, on the other hand . . .

Rule No. 139: The best food comes from good-quality ingredients combined with a simple approach. Spend more time finding your chicken and less time rubbing stuff on it.

Rule No. 140: Use a metal bowl, iced beforehand, and a large whisk. Pour in heavy cream and work it in a steady, rapid, revolving movement. Bang the bowl with your whisk. Do not quit. Whipping cream into its fullest state is like growing up: You'll never know when it starts, but you'll know when you get there.

Rule No. 141: When making tomato sauce, go easy on the tomato paste. It's wickedly acidic and tilts the flavor in a dire fashion.

Rule No. 142:
There is nothing worse than a mealy, flavorless, out-of-season tomato.

Rule No. 143:

If you can't decide whether meat smells bad, it does.

Rule No. 144: Better rum than sugar. **Rule No. 145:** Chervil is underrated—as an herb and as a first name. **Rule No. 146:** Browner! **Rule No. 147:** A ripe avocado dictates the menu for the next meal. After that, it's too late. **Rule No. 148:** Corn needs salt in the water. Not much. **Rule No. 149:** Fresh herbs make everything taste fresher, even if it is only a frozen dinner. Snip them with scissors.

Rule No. 150: Nobody cares how you made it.

Rule No. 151:
Hamburgers need salad on them like salads need a bun.

Rule No. 153:
A man should always be ready, willing, and able to make a batch of guacamole without a written recipe. The essentials: Ripe avocados, lime, salt. You can probably figure out the proportions. Onions, tomatoes, and cilantro are probably essential, too.

Rule No. 154:

Kale, salmon, red wine, a root vegetable. These are the elemental foods. The foundation of cooking. Master techniques for all four—steaming, broiling/grilling, pairing, and roasting—and you will begin to know what it takes to cook.

Rule No. 155: Of all the food that comes from the ocean, mussels are the easiest to cook.

Rule No. 156:
Substitute. Improvise. Don't be a slave to the recipe. Sour cream and yogurt are pretty similar, if you think about it. And if they want you to sauté onions, shallots, and garlic and you only have onions and garlic, you will be okay. Relax.

Rule No. 157:
Salads take the longest.

Rule No. 158: A bacon slice shouldn't be stiff and it shouldn't be supple. If you can break it or fold it in half, it hasn't been cooked right.

Rule No. 159: Cook tough things slow, tender things fast, and use plenty of salt either way.

Rule No. 160:

A spoon of cream goes further than a gallon of skim.

Rule No. 161: There are never too many napkins or too many potatoes.

Rule No. 162: Never use your fingers to taste the sauce. You might have to taste it again with the finger you licked. Use a spoon.

Rule No. 163: Not everything needs pepper.

Rule No. 165:

Have a signature go-to breakfast.

Rule No. 166: Remember, the cook usually gets away without having to clean. If you are he, protest once, then slowly back out of the room.

Rule No. 167: Have a good, large, heavy cutting board as a headquarters of operations. A few layers of damp paper towel underneath will keep it from sliding around.

Rule No. 168:
Spices like heat. Add them at the beginning. Herbs don't. Add them toward the end.

Rule No. 169:

When serving wine, save the best for first.

Rule No. 170:

Two words: *Slow cooker.*

Rule No. 171:

Soak raw onions for sandwiches in very cold water to reduce their potency.

Rule No. 172: Properly made leftover chili gets better and better every day until the fourth day, at which point it begins to decline.

Rule No. 173:

You need to be able to open a beer bottle with at least three different implements, all within arm's reach always: Spoon, tongs, knife.

Rule No. 174:

Never teeth, however. Even if you can. It makes people very uncomfortable.

Rule No. 175:

Keep it moist.

 **Rule No. 176:** Frozen cod is something they serve in school cafeterias. Fresh cod is unbearably good.

Rule No. 177:

Salt, pepper; onion, garlic; olive oil, lemon. All you need.

Rule No. 178:
Save leftover bacon fat for a rainy day.

Rule No. 179:
There is no need to add milk to your scrambled eggs. *Repeat:* There is no need to add milk to your scrambled eggs.

Rule No. 180:
The most important thing in chili is not the meat or the beans. The most important thing in chili is the chili powder.

Rule No. 181:
Save some of the starch-enriched pasta cooking water to simmer into your sauce for a better texture.

Rule No. 182:

After you brown meat in a pan, always use that pan for something else—cooking onions or building a sauce. Flavor!

Rule No. 183:

Wear gloves when handling chiles. The oils get on your fingers and can irritate your skin and, when you touch your eyes, make you feel as if you're going blind.

Rule No. 184: Aside from rare exceptions that start with the word Cajun, black is a bad color for food.

Rule No. 185: Lemon juice in a vinaigrette instead of vinegar.

Rule No. 186:
Assembling a big spread of charcuterie, cheeses, and accompaniments for a hungry crowd is cooking, too.

Rule No. 187:
That being said, forgo the expensive charcuterie.

Rule No. 188:
Charcuterie is cured meat on wood. Get a cutting board. Put some cured meat on it. Charcuterie.

Rule No. 189: Food stays good for a while, until it doesn't.

Rule No. 190:

Pope's nose is the funniest part.

Rule No. 191:

The only thing in the kitchen that should cook at a boil is pasta.

Rule No. 192:

Sous vide is for having more time to talk to your guests.

Rule No. 193: Sous vide is not for talking about sous vide with your guests.

Rule No. 194:
A universal rule: Might as well make enough for leftovers. Is there anything you can't make into a sandwich? **Rule No. 195:** Fresh fish doesn't smell like fish; it smells like the ocean. **Rule No. 196:** Garlic tastes better when it melts into food. Slice, don't chop. **Rule No. 197:** If it's not a fried egg, you shouldn't be eating it scalding hot. **Rule No. 198:** Because if something tastes good hot, it will taste better warm.

Rule No. 199: One great knife is better than a whole set of good ones.

Rule No. 200:
A good butcher is your greatest ally. He contains multitudes. Use him to the utmost.

Rule No. 201:

Keep your chocolate dark.

Rule No. 202: You can always fool them with butter. **Rule No. 203:** Let someone else bring dessert. **Rule No. 204:** "Done" is a solipsism. A metaphysical construct. **Rule No. 205:** Use a thermometer.

Rules No. 206–208:

What expiration labels actually mean

> "Sell by"

The product will be safe to eat or drink for some time after this date.

> "Best if used by"

Safe to eat after this date, but won't taste as good or have as much nutritional value as fresh food.

> "Use by"

Chuck it past this date.

Rule No. 209:
The Red Delicious: always red, rarely delicious.

THINGS EVERY MAN NEEDS TO KNOW ABOUT EATING IN PUBLIC

Rule No. 210: A waiter who takes your order by tablet is approximately half a waiter.

Rule No. 211: Don't eat lobsters over two pounds. The bigger they get, the worse they get. And never order lobster tails, which are almost always frozen.

Rule No. 212: The right way to hold a coffee cup is as follows: ring finger on the bottom, thumb on the top.

Rules No. 213–215: When dining alone, text as much as you like. • When dining with acompanion, wait until he or she goes to the restroom. • In either case, don't talk on the phone, ever, for any reason.

Rule No. 216: Don't lecture servers or make a point of announcing trophy allergies. Don't bellow, guffaw, high-five, or yell "Woo!" Don't ask waiters to take your picture, charge your phone, or box up your seven uneaten Brussels sprouts. Be cool.

Rule No. 217: If on your journey you should encounter a misspelled sign on the side of the road advertising fruit, buy some.

Rule No. 218:
Half-price burritos are never a great idea.

Rule No. 219: Minty refreshment notwithstanding, the loose candy in a bowl next to the diner cash register should be avoided, mini-tongs or no.

Rule No. 220:
Tip a minimum of 20 percent in a ritzy restaurant and 25 percent in a casual one. Whether or not you had to wait. Whether or not you thought the service up to snuff. Whether or not you feel like it. Have you ever waited tables?

Rule No. 221:
You don't need to sample
the soup, because the soup
will almost invariably
taste like soup.

Rule No. 222:
You can sample
the ice cream.

Rule No. 223: Split the bill, by all means. But don't ask to have it divided in a way that requires the use of Fourier series or irrational numbers. **Rule No. 224:** At a restaurant, check-paying responsibilities may be conceded only after saying "Allow me" followed by an "I insist" and then a "Come on!"

Rule No. 225: Saying "Allow me" without actually reaching for the check does not suggest sincerity.

Rules No. 226–230:
How to split the bill

> **With friends:**
Evenly. Always.

> **On business:**
The inviter pays.

> **First date:**
Man pays.

> **Fifth date:**
Man pays, unless otherwise mutually agreed upon.

> **With parents or in-laws:**
Let them pay.

Rule No. 231:
Never the crumble. Sometimes the crisp. Always the cobbler.

Rule No. 232: In a bar, or a diner, when you have a choice: Face the door, not the TV. Better stories.

Rule No. 233:
If a child under the age of ten is selling it, then you have to buy it.

Rule No. 234:
At a diner, never order something that involves a sauce that ends in -*aise*.

Rule No. 235:
Order seafood in a seafood restaurant, and steak in a steakhouse, and vegetables in a farm-to-table place.

Rule No. 236:
Unless you are a jaded gastronome or a weirdo, avoid savory desserts like the plague they are.

Rule No. 237: Sharing a dessert is no way to end a meal.

Rule No. 238: That said, when sharing a dessert, know no boundaries.

Rule No. 239: Watermelon is the least faithful artificial flavor.

Rule No. 240: A sandwich tastes exactly one-third better when it's made by someone else.

Rule No. 241:
The three most important words to say in a diner: "extra, extra crispy."

Rule No. 242: Beware the restaurant where the waiter steers you toward the burger.

Rule No. 243: Related: No matter how "killer" the mac and cheese is purported to be, it will be, invariably, pretty good.

Rule No. 244:

When an item in a vending machine is teetering on the precipice, it must be dislodged.

Rule No. 245: . . . But only by purchasing the product above it.

Rule No. 246: . . . Unless the product in question is baked chips.

Rule No. 247: There isn't a hunger that baked chips can satisfy.

Rule No. 248: Cheez-Its, obviously, are the ideal.

Rule No. 249:
When a waitress in a breakfast joint puts her hand on your shoulder or reaches out to tuck in the tag on your sweater, it is a gift.

Rule No. 250:
Don't keep lists of what you don't like. Keep lists of what you haven't liked yet.

Rule No. 251:
It's impossible to drink a gallon of milk without pausing to vomit.

Rule No. 252:
The foods you couldn't stand as a boy all turn out to be great. Corned-beef hash. Herring in cream sauce. Collard greens. Kale. Rye crisps. Lox. Field peas.

Rule No. 253: Always ask for a recommendation; don't always take it.

Rule No. 254:

No joke you thought of in the restaurant bathroom is worth bringing back to the table.

Rule No. 255: Especially if it's a witty take on how "employees must wash hands."

Rule No. 256: The cardboard coffee sleeve at the café should be employed only in the most treacherous of conditions and discarded at the earliest opportunity.

Rules No. 257–260:
How to wait for a table

> ## First, decide if it's worth it.

> Staying? Okay. Then relax.
> Have a drink. Remind your date how beautiful she
> is. Have another drink. Unless you're alone, PDA
> stays in your pocket.

> Feel free to politely ask the host how it's looking if
> you've been waiting longer than expected. But don't
> badger the host every 2.8 minutes.

> If your date is the one doing the badgering . . .
> you should find a new date, lest you feel like that
> host for life.

Rule No. 261:
Of all the ethnic
restaurants, Indian places
are the least likely
to have enough room
on the table.

Rule No. 262:
When in doubt,
go with the
lamb biryani.

Rule No. 263:
The prix fixe menu will involve a crappy dessert.

Rule No. 264:
There are wonderful strawberries and great cantaloupes, but there is no such thing as an unusually good banana.

Rule No. 265:
Your fruit salad will have too much melon.

Rule No. 266:
Less amuse, more bouche.

Rule No. 267: It is impossible to describe the taste of good goat cheese.

Rules No. 268-271:
Can I send my order back?

> Is it clearly over or undercooked? Yes.

> Did the waiter mishear? Yes.

> Your date doesn't like her dish: Of course. That's horrible, we'll get you a new one right away.

> You just don't like it: Tough shit.

CHAPTER 4

THE RULES OF

WORKING

GETTING A JOB
HAVING A JOB
HANDLING A BOSS
UNDERLINGS

GETTING A JOB

Rule No. 272:

It is never a mistake to wear a suit and tie to a job interview. Even if you're applying to be a mechanic.

Rule No. 273: Also: shoes that were shined that day.

Rule No. 274: Don't be late. But don't be too early, either. Six minutes, max. Any more and you become an interrupting weenie.

Rule No. 275: What to carry: a notebook, and a pen in your breast pocket; your résumé (even if they already have it); mints; a little confidence.

Rule No. 276: There is never a good reason to bring a briefcase to a job interview.

Rule No. 277:
Stand, don't sit, in the waiting area. Less fussing with yourself when they come to retrieve you.

Rule No. 278:
If it's not obvious where you should sit for the interview, just ask. Try something like, "Where's a good place for me to sit?"

Rule No. 279:
When you speak, tread in the waters that lie between the shores of braggadocio and self-deprecation.

Rule No. 280:
Which means that you can toot your own horn a little. Never assume someone has memorized your résumé. Or looked at it.

Rule No. 281: The same day: Mail a thank-you note. In the mail. The actual mail.

Rules No. 282–285:
Your first day at work

> Don't bring doughnuts. Yet.
(See Rule No. 293)

> Say very little. Smile a lot.

> If no one invites you to lunch, don't take it personally. Remember, for them it's just another day at the office. Ask where you can find a decent sandwich, and wash it down with your tears.

> Don't call any meetings.

HAVING A JOB

Rule No. 286:

You should slightly out-dress the boss. It keeps him on his toes.

Rule No. 287:
Nice trousers with a crease down each leg instantly raises you a pay grade.

Rule No. 288:
Instant-messaging does not look like working. But e-mailing friends and dates from your work account does.

Rule No. 289:
No matter what the activity, if you're holding a pen in your hand, it looks like you're working.

Rule No. 290:

Once in a while, read a novel. On your commute. Life is bigger than work.

Rule No. 291:
Unless you commute by car.

Rule No. 292:
Audiobooks are overrated.

Rule No. 293: Once in a while, on your way to the office, pick up a box of doughnuts for everybody.

Rule No. 294: If you spot a coworker on the bus/subway/train/sidewalk while traveling to work, a simple nod and smile will suffice. Let's savor these last moments of personal time in the morning, shall we?

Rule No. 295:

ALWAYS   SOMETIMES   NEVER

Rule No. 296:
Wearing high-quality sneakers to work before changing into dress shoes is probably really good for your feet. It also makes you look like a dorkus malorkus.

Rule No. 297: Get to know the people along the way: the garage attendant, the train conductor, the bus driver, the security guard. Someday you might be a buck short or a minute late and need a hand.

Rule No. 298: There is no shame in stopping into a bar for a quick drink on your way home. A small pour, seven minutes, nine bucks. Nobody has to know.

Rule No. 299: Related: Keep a small (375 ml) bottle of brown liquor in your desk drawer. Offer it, neat, to whomever else is working late one night. It's a small gesture that changes everything.

Rule No. 300:

Always accept the former intern's LinkedIn request—especially from the one with the serial-killer haircut. (He can't hurt you there.)

Rule No. 301:

ALWAYS   SOMETIMES   NEVER

Rules No. 302–306:
Meetings and conference calls

> **Be the first** person on the conference call. Be the second person at the meeting. > **The best way** to call a meeting is to send out an e-mail. Unless mandated, avoid auto-invites that people have to "accept" or "decline." Everybody hates those. > **If you make** a successful joke during a conference call, resist the urge to then state your name. > **Think about** how long a meeting is expected to last. Then think about whether you really need to bring a beverage to help you through it. > **Only the boss** gets to check e-mail during a meeting. During a conference call, anyone may. But type softly. And listen for your name.

Rules No. 307–312:

Regarding office romance

> **The chances of it all working out are slim.**

> That said, it happens.

> Your relationship will remain secret for no more than three weeks, no matter how hard you try— and you must try.

> The only real problem is if one of you is the other's boss. You could maybe get fired.

> Don't bring your work home with you. Conversely, no canoodling, bickering, or lovemaking at the office.

> Exit strategies are limited to a job change and marriage.

Rule No. 313:

A man should never wear a Halloween costume to work.

Rule No. 314: Unless he works at an elementary school.

Rule No. 315: In which case, he must.

Rule No. 316:
Your job is never as safe as you think it is. Especially if you're a window washer.

Rule No. 317: Take no more than one son or daughter to "Take Your Son or Daughter to Work Day."

Rule No. 318: An open-office floor plan is a revolutionary way to ensure that employees wear headphones and work silently all day.

Concerning the Men's Room

Rule No. 319:

No matter how long it's been, no shaking of hands in the men's room at work.

Rule No. 320:

ALWAYS   SOMETIMES   NEVER

Rule No. 321:

ALWAYS   **SOMETIMES**   **NEVER**

Rule No. 322:

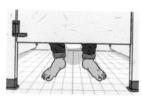

ALWAYS   **SOMETIMES**   **NEVER**

Rule No. 323:

ALWAYS   **SOMETIMES**   **NEVER**

Rules No. 324–333:
How to be a good boss

Arrive before everyone else. Look people in the eye. Everyone. But don't work hard on speaking to them. • Do not look for consensus. Ask for volunteers. When no one volunteers, do it yourself. Then ask for volunteers again.

If no one responds this time, fire someone. • **Don't touch. Don't fraternize. Don't sleep with.** • Flip through the handbook and look for rules you can undo, ignore, live without, eliminate. • **Understand: Everything is your fault.** • People want bonuses. From top to bottom. If you give bonuses, give bonuses to all. • Know that there is honor in taking care of people, in providing for their families. Treat it as an honor, and expect that your employees do the same. • You cannot answer prayers. But you can understand that cancer, death, sick parents, and tragedies on the other side of the planet knock families for a loop. • **Making things easier in times of trouble is not betraying the bottom line. It is being a good boss.** • Try to go home after everyone else.

CHAPTER 5

THE RULES CONCERNING

TRAVEL

BY CAR
BY PLANE
BY OTHER MEANS

Rule No. 334:
"Leather-wrapped."
Yes. "Leather-
appointed." Nah.

Rule No. 335:
The hands-free
technology will be
annoying to set up.

Rule No. 336:
Headlamp washers are
an emblem. And not a
good one.

Rule No. 337:
You don't need the moonroof.

Rule No. 338: No matter how many sensors they built into your car, you still have to look behind you. And to the side. And in front. Especially while the car is in motion.

Rule No. 339: Key word is *assist*.

Rule No. 340: The proper application of the blinker smooths over a multitude of sins.

Rule No. 341:

ALWAYS

SOMETIMES

NEVER

Rule No. 342:
The color of your rental car will be your least favorite car color.

Rule No. 343: Unless you are related, a candidate must be running for state office or higher to deserve a bumper sticker on your car.

Rule No. 344: The car in front of you that is just in your stinking way is either a Prius or a Subaru.

Rule No. 345:
Every city has the world's worst drivers.

Rule No. 346:
It is a miracle that more people don't get killed in parking garages by cars speeding around the corners.

Rule No. 347:
You may flip off the driver with the braggadocious vanity plate for the smallest of infractions.

Rule No. 348:
God bless the bubbly traffic reporter.

Rule No. 349:
The weigh station will be closed.

Rule No. 350: Events that are inappropriate to live-tweet: Your delay waiting to board; your delay waiting to take off; your delay waiting to disembark; your delay at the baggage carousel; the mix-up at the car-rental place; the traffic on the way home from the airport; the accident causing the traffic jam; the accident that you've just caused because you're tweeting and driving; your own death.

Rule No. 351: There's a reason the flight was cheap.

Rule No. 352: There's a 94 percent chance that, were it not for the fact of in-flight movies, you might never have seen the work or known the charms of Rachel McAdams. Choose your in-flight viewing fare accordingly.

Rule No. 353: It's never a good idea to look too deep into the seat-back pocket in front of you.

Rule No. 354:
Accept the water. Refuse the blanket.

Rule No. 355: Middle armrests: Belong to the middle seat.

Rule No. 356: Talking: Minimal, but be courteous.

Rule No. 357: Two drinks: Good for the nerves.

Rule No. 358: Three drinks: You'll forget the cattle in the row ahead.

Rule No. 359: Four-plus drinks: You might end up on YouTube.

Rule No. 360: When the pilot begins the announcement with "Well, folks," it will not be good news.

Rule No. 361:

ALWAYS

SOMETIMES

NEVER

Rule No. 362:
Treat flight attendants with respect. "Please" and "Thanks" cost nothing to say.

Rule No. 363:
You are *flying*. Thousands of feet in the air. In a *giant metal tube*. Would it kill you to show a little wonder?

Rule No. 364:

Just because your seat back reclines doesn't mean you must lean back all the way, especially in coach.

Rule No. 365: The Wi-Fi won't work.

Rule No. 366: Horse-drawn-carriage rides are actually—and in almost every respect—the least romantic mode of transport.

Rule No. 367: It is impossible to walk in a perfectly straight line while looking at your smartphone.

Rule No. 368:

No moseying.

Rule No. 369: On the bus or train, do not block the door. If you don't want to hold the pole, you probably already carry sanitizer. Use it. **Rule No. 370:** Ladies sit. **Rule No. 371:** Talking: never with strangers; quietly with acquaintances.

Rule No. 372: When walking, be swift. No weaving. No giant umbrellas. No groups of more than two across. By all means, use your smartphone. Just don't expect people to move out of the way for you.

Rule No. 373: As a gait, ambling is underrated.

Rule No. 374: Women enter the elevator first. Look straight ahead. No phone calls. No talking to others unless spoken to. Even then, keep it brief. And we know you're in a rush, but don't crazily hit the close button as if you're about to piss your pants. It's annoying.

Rule No. 375: If the person next to you on the bus or in the elevator stares at you for what feels like a moment too long—like you might have something on your face—it's because he or she can hear the music coming out of your headphones.

Rule No. 376: No matter your mode of transportation, the consumption of food and drink while commuting is rarely smooth. Eat at home. You're not saving any time.

Rules No. 377–378:

ALWAYS

SOMETIMES

NEVER

Rule No. 379: The only way to say "Thanks" to the folks who clean your hotel room is with a ten-dollar or twenty-dollar bill left on the night table just before you check out.

Rule No. 380: Even if room service does add an automatic tip, a couple of bucks won't hurt you. Same goes for the parking valet.

Rule No. 381: Hotel rooms look 30 percent more inviting online than they do in person.

Rule No. 382: All shower-curtain rods should be like the curved ones for fuller-figured guests at the Sheraton.

Rule No. 383: There is never something so urgent that you have to pass others on a single-width escalator.

Rule No. 384: That said, it's not a ride. Keep moving.

RULES OF A MORE GENERAL NATURE

Rules No. 385–403:

Things that are supposed to feel good but don't so much

Hammocks • Airplane pillows • **Water beds** • Thanksgiving dinner • Aloe vera • Winning at Ping-Pong • Meeting new people • Helping out at the soup kitchen • Fake breasts • **Great-grandmother's kisses** • Recycling • The laugh of a child • Finishing *War and Peace* • A friend's success • Saving money at Men's Wearhouse • **Running** • "Getting back out there" • An old man's blithesome whistling • **"I love you"**

Rule No. 404: It is impossible for any of the following events to live up to your expectations: Your first day of high school; prom; losing your virginity; buying your first home; being your own boss; death.

Rule No. 405:

In general, avoid the last thing: The last subway car, the last deviled egg, the last woman in the bar, etc.

Rule No. 406: Related: Avoid being the last to leave the party.

Rule No. 407: Most fun new thing to shop for: A car. Rule No. 408: Least fun new thing to shop for: A cell phone.

Rules No. 409–412:

Things a man should not do in public

> Check Facebook.

> Argue with a woman.

> Clip his nails.

> Order a drink named after a sexual position.

Rules No. 413–415: Things that are supposed to feel good that actually do:
- The backscratcher • A hug from a large woman • Moleskin trousers

CHAPTER 6

THE RULES REGARDING

STYLE

CULTIVATION OF WARDROBE
APPROPRIATE ATTIRE
POTENTIAL DISASTERS

DRESSING WELL

Rule No. 416:

Swim trunks should be the only thing in a man's wardrobe that could be described as "fun."

Rule No. 417: Clothes that could be worn in the gym should not be worn on an airplane. Unless you're the champion. Or an old lady. Or both.

Rule No. 418:
That single earring is not doing for the middle-aged gentleman's image what the middle-aged gentleman thinks it's doing.

Ten Essential Truths
of Men's Style

by *Esquire*'s Fashion Director, Nick Sullivan

Rule No. 419: If you like something, respect it. Hang your pants. Roll your ties. Put shoe trees in your shoes. Oh, and wire hangers? The instruments of Beelzebub and, coincidentally, dry cleaners. Stick with wooden ones.

Rule No. 420: The best way to look effortless is to work hard at it.

Rule No. 421: Most people, most of the time, judge you by what you're wearing, and if you care what people think, you should care about what you wear. Life doesn't get much simpler than that.

Rule No. 422: Pull yourself together. Always. Everywhere. Whether you're going to the deli or on a date, every occasion has minimum standards. Try to meet them.

Rule No. 423: People who are slaves to matching (e.g., belts to shoes, socks to trousers) are shallow and tend to lack in the friends department. Anyone points out that something doesn't match? Punch him. That'll teach him.

Rule No. 424: Never attempt maintenance, home improvement, house moving, or gardening in any of your best pieces of clothing. You are only asking for trouble.

Rule No. 425: Your posture is half the investment in buying a new suit. If you're not going to stand up straight, you might as well wear a Hefty bag.

Rule No. 426: Fit is the other half. Money is only a minor consideration.

Rule No. 427: Check your fly.

Rule No. 428: Learn to sew a button. It's a life-changing skill that teaches you patience and the value of self-sufficiency. We cannot say the same about knitting.

Rule No. 429: The length of your trousers is everything. A half inch too long and you're instantly disreputable; a half inch too short and you're laughable. A one-inch kink in the front crease and you, my friend, are golden.

Rule No. 430: The longer a presidential candidate's necktie, the bleaker his prospects.

Rule No. 431: Leave the conspicuously thick sweaters to the Irish fishermen.

Rule No. 432: With a good pair of gloves, a man can do anything.

Rule No. 433: With a good pair of mittens, a man is pretty much helpless.

Rule No. 434: The least helpful clothing-care instructions are the ironing suggestions on underwear.

Rule No. 435:

ALWAYS   SOMETIMES   NEVER

Rule No. 436:

A great cobbler is the closest thing in the world to a good wizard.

Rule No. 437: The hardest temperature to dress appropriately for is 48 degrees.

Rule No. 438:

ALWAYS

SOMETIMES

NEVER

Rules No. 439–445:
About those socks

> The man wearing bright-red socks deserves whatever's coming to him.

> **That said, nice socks, buddy.**

> Most people who say "nice socks" do not mean it.

> **The platonic ideal** of the black sock should be absorbent, fade-resistant, and retain elasticity so long as you both shall live. This sock does not exist.

> You can tell a lot about a guy by his socks. Like what kinds of socks he wears.

> **Black socks:** with everything.
Navy socks: with everything but black pants.
White socks: only when ballin'.

> **The optimal combination:** 80 percent mercerized cotton for softness and absorption, 20 percent nylon for stretch.

Rule No. 446:

ALWAYS   SOMETIMES   NEVER

Rules No. 447–454:
Places you can and cannot wear shorts

> **Yes:** A golf course
> **No:** The White House (unless your last name is Obama)
> **No:** A restaurant that does not have a patio next to a body of water
> **Yes:** A restaurant that does
> **No:** The office
> **No:** A summer wedding
> **No:** A bar after dark
> **Yes:** A bar during the day

SHOPPING

Rule No. 455:
Try it on.

Rule No. 456: The louder the music, the less helpful the sales staff.

Rule No. 457: Before purchasing a suit at a store with "Mart," "Emporium," "Barn," or "O-Rama" in its name: Don't.

Rule No. 458: "I'll think about it" are the four most useful words in a man's shopping vocabulary.

Rule No. 459: Things you can always buy without trying on: T-shirts, underwear, socks. Things you can *never* buy without trying on: Everything else.

Rule No. 460:
There is no honor in buying something with the intention of later returning it.

Rule No. 461:
Store credit is bullshit.

Rule No. 462:
There's a reason it's on sale.

Rule No. 463: Fall clothes arrive in early August. (Mostly.) Spring clothes arrive in early February. (Mostly.) These are the best times to buy last season's stuff on sale.

Rule No. 464: A well-built shopping bag is a thing of beauty.

Rule No. 465: Some companies may be tempted to offer an online feature that allows men to upload photos of themselves for the purpose of trying on items in a digital dressing room before purchasing said items. Those companies should know those features will not work. **Rule No. 466:** The later in the day you shop for shoes, the more swollen your feet and the worse the fit.

Rule No. 467: The better you're dressed, the better the service.

Rule No. 468:

ALWAYS

SOMETIMES

NEVER

Rule No. 470: Things a man should not buy online: fishing rods, bed sheets, plants, jeans.

Rule No. 471: Things a man should buy online: everything else, assuming a decent return policy.

Rule No. 472: You did check the return policy, right?

Rule No. 473: When ordering a custom shirt online, the more measurements you are asked to enter, the worse the resulting shirt will fit.

Rule No. 474: Things cashiers should stop asking: whether we want to save 10 percent by applying for a credit card today; whether we are "in their system"; whether anybody helped us today.

Rule No. 475: No matter one's context or intended keeping-it-realness, answering that last question with "the black guy" is at best insensitive and at worst racist.

Rule No. 476:

ALWAYS

SOMETIMES

NEVER

Rules No. 477–481:

Custom clothing: Worth it or not worth it

> **Jeans?** Not worth it.

> **Shirt?** Worth it.

> **Sneakers?** Not worth it.

> **Dress shoes?** Worth it.

> **Suit?** Depends.

If you have the money (typically mid-four-figures) and the time (multiple fittings over many weeks) to get fitted for a custom suit: By all means. If you have neither the time nor the resources: You'll be fine with off-the-rack.

CHAPTER 7

THE RULES PERTAINING TO

COMMUNICATION

HOW
WHY
WHEN
TO WHOM

Rule No. 482: One should text "LOL" only if you laughed out loud so hard that you broke all your fingers, making it harder to type—an odd time for laughter, to be honest.

Rule No. 483: It is impossible to pass people in another boat without waving.

Rule No. 484:

In an argument between two men, the one chewing a cigar naturally has the upper hand.

Rule No. 485: It is impossible to start a good story with "This morning in spin class . . ."

Rule No. 486: When a man turns 23 it's very important he stop using the word "party" as a verb.

Rule No. 487: People who habitually mark e-mails as "urgent" usually possess neither the authority to send an urgent e-mail nor the intelligence to tell the difference.

Rule No. 488: If you have been drinking, arrested, or touring a hostile land full of gun-toting fundamentalists, talk one-fifth as much as you listen.

Rule No. 489: Never trust anyone who, within five minutes of meeting you, tells you where he went to college.

Rule No. 490: If you are over six-three or under five-three, you will be asked, "How tall are you?" approximately 4,271 times before you die.

Rule No. 491: There is no dignified way to ask why you weren't invited to the pool party.

Rule No. 492:
The quickest way to impress twins is to be able to tell which is which.

Rule No. 493:
The quickest way to impress triplets is to not spend ten minutes discussing the fact that they're triplets.

Rule No. 494:
Do not antagonize a man with an eye patch.

Rule No. 495:
You look 12 percent more important wearing a hands-free headset.

Rule No. 496:
But only when standing.

Rule No. 508: When one finds oneself embroiled in an internet feud, the best tone to take is withering patronization. Next best is a reasoned, well-documented, possibly footnoted rebuttal. Last resort is some threat of mindless violence. Threats of mindless violence should be reserved for places where we used to gather: Taverns, parks, hockey arenas, sewing circles.

Rule No. 509: At this point, you can no longer blame autocorrect.

Rule No. 510: Luddites never prosper. Adapt or perish.

Rule No. 511:

You do not have to respond to any e-mail sent after the end of work hours until the next workday morning because you are a human being with a soul.

Rule No. 512: Life is too short to question another man's time-saving use of *u* instead of you.

Rule No. 513: Really, though: *u*?

Rule No. 514:
Your moral stance on the racial makeup of emojis is misplaced if you have not acted upon a similar stance about the racial diversity of television and children's-book characters.

Rule No. 515: When sent alone, this is the most disturbing emoji:

Rule No. 516:
It is not rude for one to ask to be removed from a group text that one is no longer involved in.

Rule No. 517:
It is, however, rude to ask to be removed from a group text with your family members.

Rule No. 518:
Especially when planning a funeral.

Rule No. 519: The use of the expression "Good gravy!" invalidates your alarm.

Rule No. 520: Unless you're talking about some really good gravy, then by all means.

Rule No. 521: In ascending order of aggravation: extravagant use of the French language (*je ne sais quoi*, whatever *du jour*); extravagant use of pop-culture references ("Not that there's anything wrong with that"); extravagant use of abbreviations (obvs, totes, abbreves).

Rule No. 522: "Hey, stranger" doesn't work on actual strangers.

Rule No. 523: The plate of the guy who says his plate is too full is no more full than anybody else's plate. All the plates are full. We all have full plates.

Rules No. 524–530: Things a man should never say to a police officer **>** Would you mind holding this? **>** Hi! **>** What do you got there—a truncheon? **>** Somebody didn't say "please." **>** Pow **>** Easy there, Tackleberry. **>** Be with you in two shakes.

Rule No. 531:

That said, god bless the fun cop.

Rule No. 532: If your lawyer's e-mail address ends in hotmail.com, gmail.com, or yahoo.com, find a new lawyer.

Rule No. 533: You can say "frickin' " and you can say "frackin'," but you can't say "frickin' frackin'."

Rule No. 534: Regards, in descending order of sincerity: Kind, warm, kindest, warmest, best.

Rule No. 535: Rarely titter. Never snigger.

Rule No. 536: The simper is the most underrated of facial expressions.

Rule No. 537:

Always the smile. Sometimes the nod. Never the wink.

Rules No. 538–541: It is possible to be honest on Yelp without being an asshole.

> Instead of "terrible," try "unsatisfying."
> Instead of "incompetent," try "slow."
> Instead of "idiot," try "inattentive."
> Instead of "It sucked," try "I wouldn't recommend it."

Rule No. 542: When speaking of e-mailing, do not pantomime typing.

Rule No. 543: Any message conveyed via purple ink is to be disregarded.

Rule No. 544:
Calling someone a "better-looking version" of someone else is not a compliment.

Rule No. 545:
You might say "so forth," or you might say "so on," but unless you're over 60, you don't say "so forth and so on."

Rule No. 546:
Whenever someone says "I'm not trying to be difficult," what will follow is a measure of difficulty that one has to try very hard to achieve.

Rule No. 547: You undermine a bit of your own authority when you address someone while eating a mini muffin.

Rule No. 548: For doctors at televised press conferences, the next two days are always critical.

Rule No. 549: Anyone who says "Blessed" in response to "How are you?" should immediately be antagonized.

Rule No. 550: Under no circumstances should your yawn be audible.

Rule No. 551: Unless you're trying to make a point.

Rule No. 552: The only possible point being that you're an extremely sleepy asshole.

Rule No. 553: Anything you do or say right before you take a sip of coffee will be rendered smug.

Rule No. 554: When there's the good news and there's the bad news, what you're exclusively dealing with is the bad news.

Rule No. 555:
Never Google Image search a word ending in *-osis*.

Rule No. 556:
Never do anything that would require a press conference to apologize for.

Rule No. 557:
No matter how tempting, e-mails from unknown people with the subject line "Hi babe!" are not to be opened.

Rule No. 558:

"I consider him a friend" does not a statement of true friendship make.

Rule No. 559: Telling them that so-and-so sent you is usually more awkward than so-and-so indicated it would be.

Rule No. 560: Tapping, in ascending order of offensiveness: A keg, a maple tree, a phone, "that ass," your pen against a table during a meeting.

Rule No. 561:
Referring to stuff as "gear" makes you seem
38 percent more capable.

Rules No. 562–635:
Words and phrases
a man should
never say

Samesies!

Note to self

Them's the rules

Show me what
you got

At least it's Friday

Put a bug in
your ear

So you think
you can dance

Doing it for
the kids

I like what I'm
seeing

Love you more

"Free Bird"

Gather 'round

The American
people

**The healing
process**
(*for anything other
than a physical
injury*)

Fallout
(*for anything other
than the nuclear
kind*)

Ditto

An acronym for
anything you
would never say in
real life

An acronym
for anything you
would say in
real life

The old heave-ho

Yuck

Easy does it

Crunch time

The road to the
White House

Yikes

My good man

Left in a huff

This will lead to
Sharia Law

Eesh

Reach out
(*unless you're talking
about actually
reaching out . . .
with your arm*)

Panties
("*underwear*"
does the trick)

Tummy

Veggie

Vino
(*Unless you're an
Italian. In Italy.*)

Natch (*as opposed
to "naturally"*)

Wingin' it
("*wing it" is fine*)

Nippy

The first name
of any female
celebrity when
you don't follow it
with her last name

Belly button
("*navel" is just fine*)

Derring-do

Going forward

It is what it is

Boobs

Teens

Slacks
("*pants" or
"trousers"*)

Expresso

Willy-nilly

Make love

Yell-o!
(*the phone greeting*)

If I may be so bold

Hooray

Toot your own
horn

March to the
beat of a different
drummer

Wunderbar
(*does not apply to
the Germans*)

Magnifico
(*does not apply to
the Italians*)

Rad

Nestled

Fingerlickin'

Right-o

Ergo

Thrice

Bleep
(*in place of a
profanity*)

Fourthly

How ya like me
now?

Bejesus

Six of one, a half
dozen of the other

First off, I'd like
to thank Jesus

Sake to me

Ex-squeeze me

**Hummina
hummina
hummina**

Hark

Lo

Mommy

_____ much?

Bye-bye

Rule No. 636:
Men who go by William would be slightly more popular if they went by Bill.

Rule No. 637:
Men who go by Gary would be slightly more popular if they went by Bill.

Rule No. 638:
Rarely frown.

Rule No. 639:
No additional valuable information comes from the question-and-answer session.

Rule No. 640: Leave the first-initial/middle-name/last-name thing to the pretentious authors.

Rule No. 641: Men in the South are much more likely to talk to one another in restrooms.

Rule No. 642: The menace you convey when holding a chainsaw has more to do with facial expression than you might think.

Rule No. 643: Of the various factors, "wow" is the most overrated.

Rule No. 644: Use of the third person, in descending order: the man who refers to himself by his first and last names, the man who refers to himself by his last name only, the man who refers to himself as "this guy right here."

Rule No. 645: You are allowed to "battle" only an army or cancer. There's no battling of other things. Not the flu. Not a crossword. Not a housefly.

Rule No. 646: Without Nantucket, there would be no limericks.

Rule No. 647: There's no good reason for a man to raise his hand after college.

Rules No. 648–686:
Further guidance on the usage of popular words and phrases

Like: Makes you sound younger than you are. Use only when it's necessary to make a complete sentence. Unless . . .

Like hell: Useful.

Awesome: Too vague, and it debases you and whatever you're praising. Consider alternatives, such as "portentous" or "sublime" or "unfuckingbelievable."

Unfuckingbelievable: This and similar conjugations are highly encouraged, e.g.,

outgoddamnrageous, insonofabitchingsane, etc.

Goddammit: If handled correctly, the most cathartic of the profanities.

Man: Highly useful as a means to temper emotion: "I'm afraid she's cheating on you, man," or "I always considered you a special friend, man."

Bro: No.

Balls: Underrated as an exclamation: "Balls!"

Sweet: Only when talking about food.

Shit: Never "shoot."

-eroo: Encouraged. It makes anything seem more fun in the telling: switcheroo, eateroo, sexeroo, arresteroo.

Buddy: Leave "buddy" to the college students and men named Buddy. Men have "friends."

Tits: Encouraged.

Piss: Three better euphemisms for urination: "make the bladder gladder," "punish the porcelain," "shake hands with an old friend."

Ma'am: Only for your girlfriend's mother. Or a female customer-service representative you need on your side.

Pussy: But not about the thing itself.

Baby: For significant other, "sweetheart." For infant, "ankle biter." If the infant's parents are around, "precious angel."

Asshole: See "son of a bitch."

Son of a bitch: See "asshole."

-tard: Says more about you than whomever you're insulting.

Rat's ass: Or "rooster's ass." Or "badger's ass."

Rathole: Useful term for inadequate lodging.

Mouthbreather: The most elegant synonym for "yokel."

Wasted: Other, better synonyms for drunk: ossified, pifflicated, plonked, plotzed, polluted, activated, bajanxed, bewottled, bruised, comboozelated, corned, electrified, fractured, honed, lathered, pafisticated, parboiled, pickled, put to bed with a shovel, scammered, schnoggered, soggy, steamed up, swozzled, walking on rocky socks, zunked. Also, drunk.

Little shit: Reserved for a misbehaving male between the ages of three and sixteen. Or a particularly aggravating younger male shorter than, say, five-seven.

Fuck: Not too much. Unless too much is the only way.

Bitch: Overrated as an insult.

Douchebag: Retired by *Esquire*, July 2008.

Dude: Also retired.

Yo: Instead of "dude!"

Yup: Preferred spelling for "yes." See also: probly (probably), lemme (let me), hijinx (high jinks).

Jesus Christ: God bless him.

Jesus H. Christ: A lot more fun "Jesus Christ."

The ol' how's your father: One of the more amusing and discrete euphemisms for sex. A few others: Cleaning the gutters, engaging in arts and crafts, tending the garden, a good rogering.

Colder than a witch's tit: Remains the most humorous of the multitude of euphemisms for "really damn cold."

Bullshit: Or "horseshit." Or "roostershit" or "badgershit." Any animal, really.

Batshit: Should always precede the word "crazy" or any synonym for "crazy": Loco, insane, meshuga, derranged, cuckoo, psycho, unhinged, touched.

Paesan: Helps diffuse an argument with a stranger whom you know to be from the same motherland as yourself, especially if you're Italian.

In the zone: Things a man can find himself in, from ideal to unfortunate: the zone, the driver's seat, the groove, the saddle, the loop, the clear, the same boat, the soup, a pickle, the dark, the belly of the beast, the trenches, the hot seat, the doghouse, the gutter, the crapper.

CHAPTER 8

THE RULES CONCERNING

LEISURE

SPORT
RECREATION
STREET FIGHTS
ETC.

Rule No. 687: If it's fast, it's fun. **Rule No. 688:** If it's in the air, it's fun. **Rule No. 689:** If it's in the water, it's fun. **Rule No. 690:** If it involves a dude in wraparound sunglasses and amiable demeanor whose sole job is to make sure you don't die, it's fun.

Rule No. 691: If it involves being stuck by yourself on a hillside along a "mountain coaster" track because you didn't tell them your real weight, it is not fun.

Rule No. 692:

Things you can do in the water in descending order of appropriateness: Float, surf, urinate, wear a T-shirt, play dead.

Rule No. 693:

It is impossible to run in flip-flops.

Rule No. 694:
When all hope is lost: Board game.

Rule No. 695:
Unless you're talking Parcheesi, which is basically Candy Land for adults.

Rule No. 696:

ALWAYS

SOMETIMES

NEVER

Rules No. 697–710:
Playing: Advisable or inadvisable

> **Playing ball:** Advisable

> **Playing devil's advocate:** Advisable

> **Playing someone at his own game:** Inadvisable

> **Playing dirty:** Depends

> **Playing dumb:** Advisable

> **Playing favorites:** Inadvisable

> **Playing it safe:** Inadvisable

> **Playing hard to get:** Advisable

> **Playing hardball:** Bet your ass

> **Playing God:** Inadvisable

> **Playing fast and loose with our nation's security:** Inadvisable

> **Playing it by ear:** Advisable

> **Playing for keeps:** Fuckin' A

> **Playing football:** Inadvisable

Rule No. 711:

When doing something is actually doing nothing: tending your Instagram feed; organizing your iTunes library; masturbating.

Rule No. 712: When doing nothing is actually doing something: drinking on your couch; meditating; binge-watching a show by yourself.

Rule No. 713: That said, binge-watching a Netflix series does not a hobby make.

Rule No. 714: In the world of sports, pole-vaulting involves the most reliably attractive women per capita, followed closely by sideline reporting.

Rule No. 715:
If on your journey you encounter a hand-lettered sign for a zip line, keep going.

Rule No. 716: The middle reliever gets laid the least. Followed by the batboy.

Rule No. 717:
People who fish are very different from people who don't fish.

Rule No. 718: When in person, urges to fight should be resisted, generally. When on social media, urges to fight should be resisted, totally.

Rule No. 719:

Something changes in a man when he brings a cowbell to a sporting event.

Rule No. 720: If over the age of thirty you are involved in a "street fight," you need to assess your life's direction.

Rule No. 721: If over the age of forty you are involved in a "street fight," you need to get yourself to a hospital, because you don't look so good.

CHAPTER 9

THE RULES OF

GROOMING

KNUCKLE HAIR
ARM HAIR
HEAD HAIR
ETC.

Rule No. 722: No man should use a product applied via mask.

Rule No. 723: Especially if it's spelled "masque."

Rule No. 724: The running of the fingers through the hair: only if you're in a dandruff commercial.

Rule No. 725:
There is no shame in moisturizer.

Rule No. 726: Eye cream, however, you may not want to leave out on your counter.

Rule No. 727: All this pressure to groom your entire body? Give in to a little bit of it.

Rule No. 728: A very little bit.

Rule No. 729: Seriously, just enough to show you care.

Rule No. 730: And your armpits are completely off-limits.

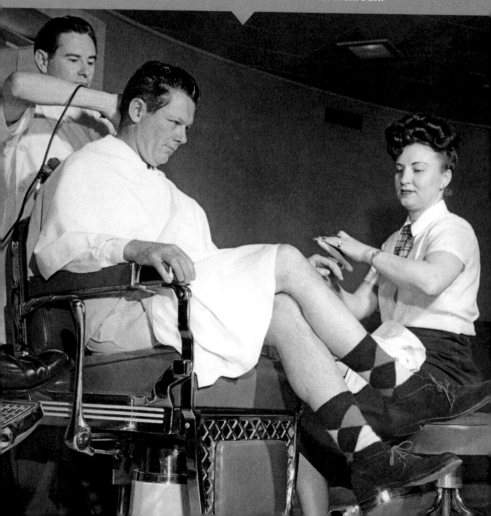

Rule No. 733: When you choose to grow a beard, you're making a commitment—to trim (at least twice a week), to wash (at least once a day), and not to be surprised when parents hide their children from you, especially if you're also wearing a ski cap.

Rule No. 734: The most important choice you make with your beard is where to end it. Never stop right at the jawline. And never let it grow like kudzu, reaching down so far that it melds with your chest hair. Find a spot somewhere between your Adam's apple and where your neck joins your head. Always taper.

Rule No. 735:

There is little chance that you smell the same as the celebrity whose cologne you just bought.

Rule No. 736: Never let another man see you apply lip balm.

Rule No. 737: Ditto hand cream.

Rule No. 738: Unless you are pitching in the World Series, there's never a good reason to dye your beard. The time for irony with facial hair is over.

Rule No. 739: If you choose to have a part, it should start no lower than the center of your eyebrow.

Rules No. 740–748: The Spa

> Taking off too little clothing is worse than taking off too much. > Even for a facial. > The more you paid for the service, the more awkward you'll feel if you joke about receiving a happy ending. > Especially for a facial. > After disrobing, as you wait for the aesthetician to return to the room, you will try three or four different positions in an attempt to find one that doesn't feel awkward. It doesn't exist. Just settle for putting your hands by your side. > No matter how shy you may be about your body, never wear a robe into the steam room. It'll just get heavy. > There's no shame in asking for a pair of shorts to wear in the hot- and cold-water baths. > The opposite is true for the shower. > Verbal response to massage should be kept to a minimum, as should requests to "hit the undercarriage, if you don't mind."

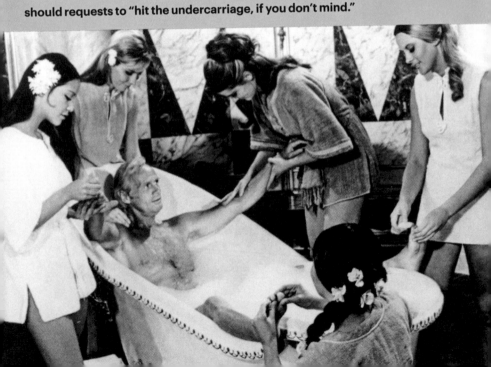

Rule No. 749: There is no shame in heroic hair-loss intervention.

Rule No. 750: Hair growth a man must always maintain: Eyebrows, nose hair, ear hair, hair on his head (if applicable).

Rule No. 751: Hair growth a man must never maintain: Arm, leg, knuckle, armpit.

Rule No. 752: Everything else: Negotiable.

Rule No. 753: Your haircut peaks for five days—and only five days—exactly one week after you have it cut.

Rule No. 754: In descending order of acceptable nomenclature: "Gel," "hair stuff," "product," "goop," "father's little helper."

Rule No. 755:

ALWAYS

SOMETIMES

NEVER

Rule No. 756:

"Makeup for men" isn't a thing. It has never been a thing. It will never be a thing.

Rule No. 757: Men with perfectly maintained facial scruff are not worthy of your trust.

Rule No. 758: In the formerly contentious and now fairly common realm of cosmetic procedures, lasers are your friends, scalpels are your enemies, and syringes are the one-night stands that you will inevitably come to regret.

Rule No. 759: Even a speck of dirt under your fingernail will repel all women.

Rule No. 760: Small circular bandages on the face raise more questions than they answer.

Rule No. 761: No, you should not get highlights.

Rule No. 762: At no age are you dismissed from looking after your eyebrows.

Rule No. 763: But don't look as though you look after your eyebrows.

CHAPTER 10

THE RULES CONCERNING

HEALTH, HYGIENE & FITNESS

IMPORTANCE OF
MAINTENANCE OF
INEVITABLE DECLINE

Rule No. 764:
Nobody cares how many steps you've taken today.

Rule No. 765: Other things nobody cares about: your WOD at your local CrossFit box, your BMI, your 10K splits, how real and authentic your disease-ridden gym is, what everyone else could be doing better at the gym.

Rule No. 766:

There is no better way to embarrass a man than to uncover and reveal the contents of his "Gym" playlist.

Rule No. 767: "Walking on Sunshine," huh?

Rule No. 768:
Any workout that allows you to read a book or complete a puzzle on your iPad while said workout is occurring is not actually a workout.

Rule No. 769:
There is a distinct difference between the way you jumped rope in grade school and the way you should do it at the gym.

Rule No. 770:
You'll know.

Rule No. 771: Some men airbrush out wrinkles and blemishes from digital photos of themselves before sharing the photos with others. Those men should stop doing that.

Rule No. 772: Profile pictures should be no more than eighteen months old.

Rule No. 773: At a certain age, you just stop having time for this nonsense.

Rule No. 774: That age is usually thirty-seven.

Rule No. 775: Grown men who open the restroom door with a paper towel are still protecting themselves against the viral infectious disease known as cooties.

Rule No. 776: If your physician prefers to be addressed as "Dr. (insert First Name here)," get a second opinion.

Rule No. 777: You don't start understanding life well until you're forty.

Rule No. 778: Upon encountering death, text your condolences but still call.

(They won't pick up. Leave a message.)

Rule No. 779: Age is an enemy in some ways but a friend in others, and people who rely on their minds should get better and smarter with age.

Rule No. 780: To a point.

Rule No. 781:

ALWAYS

SOMETIMES

NEVER

Rule No. 782: What you do is: Make a video for your kids while you still have your wits. Tell them you love them. Tell them what you need to tell them. Leave it for them to find after you die.

Rule No. 783: Try telling them those things before you die, should circumstances allow.

Rule No. 784: Prior to departing this world, prepare a document with all the passwords for your online accounts and social networks so that your next of kin can dispense with them.

Rule No. 785: Because it's the thoughtful thing to do, that's why.

Rule No. 786: "What do I care, I'll be dead soon" only really means something after you turn seventy.

Rule No. 787:

You're gonna wanna age well.

CHAPTER 11

THE RULES CONCERNING

DOMESTIC AFFAIRS

CLEANLINESS AND ORDER
COHABITATION
PARENTS AND PARENTING

LIFE AT HOME

Rule No. 788: There is no honor in fighting over the remote. Particularly if the other person is twelve.

Rule No. 789: Other things in which there is no honor: The entire fourth season of unwatched *The Walking Dead* clogging up the DVR; yelling at the television, except at the apex of a Very Big Game; food stains on the sofa cushion you usually occupy.

Rule No. 790: Water stains: no laughing matter. Coasters, or, if one isn't handy, a book or magazine.

Rule No. 791: Of the clocks in the house, the coffeemaker is the least likely to be accurate.

Rule No. 792: The scratching of one's ass is a pleasure best enjoyed outside the kitchen.

Rule No. 793: On every remote control, there is a button whose function now and forever will be a mystery.

Rule No. 794: The TV can be 10 percent quieter.

Rule No. 795:

ALWAYS

SOMETIMES

NEVER

Rule No. 796:

It is better to finish something off completely than to leave one sip of milk or the butt of the bread loaf.

Rule No. 797:
Shirt when cooking? Recommended. Pants? Required.

Rule No. 798: Past the age of four, no man should ever be caught naked from the waist down.

Rule No. 799:
Even if he's by himself.

Rule No. 800:

ALWAYS

SOMETIMES

NEVER

Rule No. 801:

Sit down to eat. Barring that, over the counter or sink. Pick up crumbs any larger than a grain of rice. Forget about the rest.

Rule No. 802: **You:** Take out garbage. Fix appliances when broken. Clear table. **Her:** Wipe down counters. Sweep floor. Clean out fridge. **Everyone:** Buy groceries. Do dishes. Cook.

Rules No. 803–826:

Regarding company

	THE DINNER PARTY	THE COCKTAIL PARTY	THE KIDS' PARTY
Ideal number of guests	Ten.	Twenty-five, mix of single and married.	Fifteen kids, three adults.
How to invite	Phone call, e-mail.	If casual, e-mail; if not, paper invitation.	Hard invites. (To be mailed or distributed at school.)
Food	Predinner: brimming antipasto plate. Dinner: light salad, main course, dessert.	Grazable plates of meats, cheese, and crudités, plus two to three plates of room-temp finger food.	Mini pizzas, pigs in a blanket, cupcakes, and/or ice-cream cake.
Drink	Five kinds of liquor (vodka, Scotch, bourbon, tequila, gin), plus mixers, soda/sparkling water, ice. Wine (more red than white).	See Dinner Party. Also: selection of cold bottled beer and pitchers of specialty cocktail, if it's that kind of party.	See Dinner Party. (Kidding!) Seriously: Under six years of age, juice boxes; over six years of age, juice and water.
Reasonable expectations for guests	To give advance notice of allergies. To refrain from ranting.	To use a coaster. To stay out of dark rooms. To keep their paws off your stuff.	To bring a present. And to share. And to listen. And to sing "Happy Birthday."
Unreasonable expectations for guests	To remove their shoes when entering your home. To bring dessert unless they volunteer to bring dessert.	To keep it down. To take care of your college friend Dave, who is completely wasted. To find karaoke as delightful as you.	To pin the tail successfully on the donkey. To clean up after themselves or behave like rational human beings.
The common problem	The couple that won't leave.	The stain on your sofa.	The bad apple.
The easy solution	Start doing the dishes, take out the trash. Last resort: Extinguish lights, head to bed.	Blot, don't scrub.	Take him/her aside and gently get to the bottom of the behavior/attitude. Or: Call the parents.

Rule No. 827:
No clothes on the floor of the bedroom. Dirty stuff in the hamper, put the rest away.

Rule No. 828: Hahaha. But seriously: Go ahead and throw your clothes on the floor, but only in the area immediately surrounding your side of the bed. Nobody will trip on them but you.

Rule No. 829:
Acceptable things to do in bed: Sleeping, reading, watching TV, having sex, and, if necessary, the discreet breaking of wind.

Rule No. 830: Unacceptable things to do in bed: Eating, smoking, clipping nails, engineering a Dutch oven for her presumed enjoyment.

Rule No. 831: One hit of the snooze button: Fine. Two hits: Really? Three or more: Dick.

Rule No. 832:

ALWAYS   **SOMETIMES**   **NEVER**

Rule No. 833: Beard whiskers in the sink, patches of toothpaste here and there: Totally fine.

Rule No. 834: **Toilet seat up. Barring that, don't piss on the seat. Barring that, wipe it up.**

Rule No. 835: Flush and, when in doubt, flush again. Light a match or, if it's there, a candle.

Rule No. 836: Brushing teeth, shaving, possibly even showering if it's just you and the missus: Door can remain ajar. Anything else: Shut it firmly.

Rule No. 837: **Showers: Under ten minutes, fifteen tops.**

THE FAMILY UNIT

Rule No. 838:

There will come a time in every man's life when it will be impossible to feel good about yourself after winning an argument with your father.

Rule No. 839: When your son brings his girlfriend home, take the girlfriend aside and tell her what a fine influence she's had on your son. It will get back to him.

Rule No. 840:
Three words:
Peanut-free
facility.

Rule No. 841: Ask not whether your children will be tattooed but which tattoos will be on your children.

Rule No. 842: Children's birthday parties are the best parties: Low expectations, obvious conversation starters, guaranteed cake.

Rules No. 843–849:
Seven things a man should give his adult son

> **Advice**, when solicited
> **A talking to**, when required
> **Help** with a down payment, when possible
> **A family heirloom** (a watch, some cufflinks), when available
> **Compliments,** intermittently
> **The benefit of the doubt**, always
> **As full a rendering** of his own life as possible, at least once

Rule No. 850:

ALWAYS

SOMETIMES

NEVER

Rule No. 851:

Really, it's not that hard.

Credits

Cover Illustrations by Joe McKendry

Alamy: © Ira Berger: 123, © Neil Fraser: 128

© Peter Arkle: 94, 106 (top strip), 119, 121, 190

© Jamie Chung: 51

© Josh Cochran: 187

Corbis: © 2/SeanMurphy/Ocean: 55

© Nigel Cox: 112

Deposit Photos: @ belchonok: 62 (raw chicken), © Jim_Filim: 23; © karandaev: 29 (viognier), © kepfish: 54; © viperagp: 62 (ice cream, milk), © zhukovsky: 154, © zoeytoja: 62 (leftovers)

Everett Collection: 92, 132 (eyepatch), 159, 166, ©Advertising Archive: 125

© F. Martin Ramin/Studio D: 160

Getty Images: ©Archive Photos: 110, © Li Kim Goh: 61, © H.Armstrong Roberts/Classicstock/Archive Photos: 165, © Rob Lawson: 29 (hot toddy), ©George Marks/Retrofile: 87, © Sean Murphy: 26, © Michael Putland/Hulton Archive: 169, © Sickles Photo Reporting: 147

iStock: © 221A: 8, © ADDRicky: 170, © adventtr: 48, © Aguru: 157, © AlexRaths: 62 (fresh fish), © cookelma: 98, © EHStock: 152, © f4f: 62 (eggs), © floortje: 62 (cooked chicken, ketchup), © Jag_cz: 24, © Joe_Potato: 68, © kyoshino: 117, © laartist: 29 (Tom Collins), © mrphillips007: 62 (steak, cooked fish), © olaser: 80, © robeo: 132 (triplets), © Rtimages: 131, © Roel Smart: 62 (ground beef), © studiocasper: 47, © WiktorD: 50, © witoldkr1: 59

© Joyce Lee: 178

©Patrick Leger: 88, 118, 167, 182, 183

© Wesley Merritt: 95 (bottom strip), 100, 155

© Mr. Bingo: 150, 151

© Mark Nerys: 11, 90, 95 (top strip), 103, 124, 126

© Marcus Nilsson: 40, 44

© Peter Oumanski: 95 (middle strip), 106 (bottom strip), 175

© Stuart Patience: 18

Shutterstock: © Everett Collection: 137, 138, 141, 144, 163

StockFood: © Glasshouse Images: 52

SuperStock: 12, 64, 96, 158, 174, © ClassicStock.com: 30, 71, © Culver Pictures, Inc.: 173